GUITAR

HAL•LEONARD
BIG BAND
PLAY-ALONG
VOLUME 7

Standards

T0078952

ISBN 978-1-4234-5886-9

HAL•LEONARD®
CORPORATION
7777 W. BLUEMOUND RD. P.O. BOX 13819 MILWAUKEE, WI 53213

Visit Hal Leonard Online at
www.halleonard.com

Standards

AUTUMN LEAVES

English lyric by JOHNNY MERCER
French lyric by JACQUES PREVERT
Music by JOSEPH KOSMA
Arranged by PETER BLAIR

GUITAR

From BORN TO DANCE

EASY TO LOVE
(YOU'D BE SO EASY TO LOVE)

Guitar

Words and Music by COLE PORTER
Arranged by SAMMY NESTICO

THIS PAGE HAS BEEN LEFT BLANK TO ACCOMMODATE PAGE TURNS.

GEORGIA ON MY MIND

Words by STUART GORRELL
Music by HOAGY CARMICHAEL
Arranged by MARK TAYLOR

HARLEM NOCTURNE

Music by EARLE HAGEN
Arranged by JOHN BERRY

From STATE FAIR

IT MIGHT AS WELL BE SPRING

Lyrics by OSCAR HAMMERSTEIN II
Music by RICHARD RODGERS
Arranged by MARK TAYLOR

Guitar

JA-DA

Words and Music by
BOB CARLETON
Arranged by SAMMY NESTICO

GUITAR

From BELLS ARE RINGING

JUST IN TIME

Words by BETTY COMDEN and ADOLPH GREEN
Music by JULE STYNE
Arranged by SAMMY NESTICO

Guitar

From BABES IN ARMS
MY FUNNY VALENTINE

Words by LORENZ HART
Music by RICHARD RODGERS
Arranged by SAMMY NESTICO

Guitar

From GOLDEN BOY
NIGHT SONG

Guitar

Lyric by LEE ADAMS
Music by CHARLES STROUSE
Arranged by RICK STITZEL

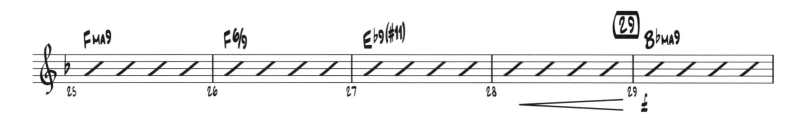

ON THE SUNNY SIDE OF THE STREET

Lyric by DOROTHY FIELDS
Music by JIMMY McHUGH
Arranged by SAMMY NESTICO

THE BIG BAND PLAY-ALONG SERIES

CD INCLUDED

HAL•LEONARD
BIG BAND
PLAY-ALONG

These revolutionary play-along packs are great products for those who want a big band sound to back up their instrument, without the pressure of playing solo. They're perfect for current players and for those former players who want to get back in the swing!

Each volume includes:

- Easy-to-read, authentic big band arrangements
- Professional recordings on CD of all the big band instruments, including the lead part
- Editions for alto sax, tenor sax, trumpet, trombone, guitar, piano, bass, and drums

1. SWING FAVORITES

April in Paris • I've Got You Under My Skin • In the Mood • It Don't Mean a Thing (If It Ain't Got That Swing) • Route 66 • Speak Low • Stompin' at the Savoy • Tangerine • This Can't Be Love • Until I Met You (Corner Pocket).

07011313	Alto Sax	$14.95
07011314	Tenor Sax	$14.95
07011315	Trumpet	$14.95
07011316	Trombone	$14.95
07011317	Guitar	$14.95
07011318	Piano	$14.95
07011319	Bass	$14.95
07011320	Drums	$14.95

2. POPULAR HITS

Ain't No Mountain High Enough • Brick House • Copacabana (At the Copa) • Evil Ways • I Heard It Through the Grapevine • On Broadway • Respect • Street Life • Yesterday • Zoot Suit Riot.

07011321	Alto Sax	$14.95
07011322	Tenor Sax	$14.95
07011323	Trumpet	$14.95
07011324	Trombone	$14.95
07011325	Guitar	$14.95
07011326	Piano	$14.95
07011327	Bass	$14.95
07011328	Drums	$14.95

3. DUKE ELLINGTON

Caravan • Chelsea Bridge • Cotton Tail • I'm Beginning to See the Light • I'm Just a Lucky So and So • In a Mellow Tone • In a Sentimental Mood • Mood Indigo • Satin Doll • Take the "A" Train.

00843086	Alto Sax	$14.95
00843087	Tenor Sax	$14.95
00843088	Trumpet	$14.95
00843089	Trombone	$14.95
00843090	Guitar	$14.95
00843091	Piano	$14.95
00843092	Bass	$14.95
00843093	Drums	$14.95

4. JAZZ CLASSICS

Bags' Groove • Blue 'N Boogie • Blue Train (Blue Trane) • Doxy • Four • Moten Swing • Oleo • Song for My Father • Stolen Moments • Straight No Chaser.

00843094	Alto Sax	$14.95
00843095	Tenor Sax	$14.95
00843096	Trumpet	$14.95
00843097	Trombone	$14.95
00843098	Guitar	$14.95
00843099	Piano	$14.95
00843100	Bass	$14.95
00843101	Drums	$14.95

5. CHRISTMAS FAVORITES

Baby, It's Cold Outside • The Christmas Song • Feliz Navidad • I'll Be Home for Christmas • Let It Snow! Let It Snow! Let It Snow! • Little Saint Nick • My Favorite Things • Silver Bells • This Christmas • White Christmas.

00843118	Alto Sax	$14.95
00843119	Tenor Sax	$14.95
00843120	Trumpet	$14.95
00843121	Trombone	$14.95
00843122	Guitar	$14.95
00843123	Piano	$14.95
00843124	Bass	$14.95
00843125	Drums	$14.95

6. LATIN

Água De Beber (Water to Drink) • At the Mambo Inn • Bésame Mucho (Kiss Me Much) • The Look of Love • Mambo No. 5 (A Little Bit of...) • Mas Que Nada • One Note Samba (Samba De Uma Nota So) • Quiet Nights of Quiet Stars (Corcovado) • Ran Kan Kan • St. Thomas.

00843126	Alto Sax	$14.99
00843127	Tenor Sax	$14.99
00843128	Trumpet	$14.99
00843129	Trombone	$14.99
00843130	Guitar	$14.99
00843131	Piano	$14.99
00843132	Bass	$14.99
00843133	Drums	$14.99

7. STANDARDS

Autumn Leaves • Easy to Love (You'd Be So Easy to Love) • Georgia on My Mind • Harlem Nocturne • It Might As Well Be Spring • Ja-Da • Just in Time • My Funny Valentine • Night Song • On the Sunny Side of the Street.

00843134	Alto Sax	$14.99
00843135	Tenor Sax	$14.99
00843136	Trumpet	$14.99
00843137	Trombone	$14.99
00843138	Guitar	$14.99
00843139	Piano	$14.99
00843140	Bass	$14.99
00843141	Drums	$14.99

FOR MORE INFORMATION,
SEE YOUR LOCAL MUSIC DEALER,
OR WRITE TO:

HAL•LEONARD®
CORPORATION
7777 W. BLUEMOUND RD. P.O. BOX 13819
MILWAUKEE, WISCONSIN 53213

www.halleonard.com

Prices, contents, and availability subject to change without notice.

0509